SUPER TASTY CROCK POT RECIPES 2021

DELICIOUS RECIPES FOR A HEALTHY LIFE

CHARLIE HUMBERT

Table of Contents

Easy Sunday Beef Sandwiches

(Ready in about 8 hours | Servings 6)

Ingredients

- 1 jar of your favourite spaghetti sauce

- 3 pounds roast meat

- 2 bay leaves

- 5-6 peppercorns

- 1 cup beef stock

- Mustard for garnish

- Pickles for garnish

Directions

1. In your crock pot, place all of the ingredients. Cook on low for 8 hours.

2. Remove bay leaves and peppercorns and ladle over English muffins.

3. Serve with mustard and pickles and enjoy!

Lazy Man's Pizza

(Ready in about 4 hours | Servings 4)

Ingredients

- 1 pound hamburger, browned and drained

- 1 pound noodles, cooked

- 2 cups mozzarella cheese, shredded

- 2 bell peppers, sliced

- 1 onion, chopped

- 1 teaspoon granulated garlic

- 1 can beef soup

- 1 cup mushrooms, sliced

- 2 jars pizza sauce

- 1/2 pound pepperoni, sliced

Directions

1. In your crock pot, alternate layers with the ingredients in the order given above.

2. Cook for 4 hours on low; then serve.

Chocolate French Toast with Honey and Bananas

(Ready in about 2 hours | Servings 6)

Ingredients

- 1 large-sized loaf bread, torn into cubes

- 2 cups low-fat milk

- 1/2 teaspoon cardamom

- 1/2 teaspoon ground cloves

- 1 teaspoon ground cinnamon

- 1 tablespoon hazelnut extract

- 5 large-sized eggs

- 2 heaping tablespoons chocolate cream, plus more for topping

- 1 tablespoon butter, unsalted

- 4 bananas, sliced

- 1 tablespoon honey

Directions

1. Put the bread cubes into your crock pot.

2. In a large mixing bowl, combine, milk, spices, hazelnut extract, eggs, and chocolate cream. Whisk well to combine.

3. Pour this mixture over the bread cubes in the crock pot to make sure the bread is well submerged.

4. Cover the crock pot with a lid and cook on high approximately 2 hours.

5. Heat a saucepan and add butter. Add bananas and honey to the hot butter and sauté 3 to 4 minutes, turning once.

6. Divide chocolate French toast among six serving plates, add banana-honey mixture and enjoy with fat-free milk!

Melt-In-Your-Mouth French Toast

(Ready in about 5 hours | Servings 8)

Ingredients

For the French Toast:

- 12-ounce loaf bread of choice

- 2 cups whole milk

- 3 eggs

- 1/2 cup brown sugar

- 1 tablespoon almond extract

- 1/4 teaspoon ground nutmeg

- 1/4 teaspoon allspice

- 1/4 teaspoon turmeric powder

- 1 teaspoon ground cinnamon

- 1 cup almonds, coarsely chopped

- 3 tablespoons unsalted butter, melted

- 2 bananas, sliced

For the Sauce:

- 1/2 cup brown sugar

- 1/2 cup half-and-half cream

- 1/2 cup butter

- 2 tablespoons corn syrup

- 1 teaspoon almond extract

Directions

1. Preheat the oven to 300 degrees F. Line a crock pot with disposable crockery liner.

2. In a baking pan, place the bread cubes in a single layer. Bake for about 15 minutes or until the bread is golden. Then, replace bread cubes to prepared crock pot.

3. In a large mixing bowl, whisk together whole milk, eggs, sugar, almond extract, nutmeg, allspice, turmeric, and cinnamon. Pour this spiced mixture over bread cubes in the crock pot. Press bread cubes down with a spoon to moisten them.

4. In a small non-stick skillet, toast the almonds for a few minutes. Combine toasted almonds with melted butter. Pour this mixture over the ingredients in the crock pot.

5. Cover, and then cook on low heat setting for about 5 hours. Remove crockery liner and set French toast aside.

6. Next, prepare the sauce. In a medium-sized saucepan, over medium-high heat, cook the ingredients for the sauce. Bring to a boil, turn the heat to low and cook for 3 more minutes.

7. You can cool prepared sauce to room temperature or set in a refrigerator. Pour the sauce over the French toast, top with banana slices and enjoy!

Homemade Yogurt with Croissants

(Ready in about 8 hours | Servings 16)

Ingredients

- 1/2 gallon low-fat milk

- 1/2 cup milk powder

- 1/4 cup plain yogurt with active yogurt cultures, at room temperature

- 16 croissants of choice

Directions

1. In a saucepan, over medium heat, combine together milk and milk powder. Cook, stirring constantly, until an instant-read thermometer registers about 180 degrees F.

2. Next, cool at room temperature

3. In a bowl, combine together 1 cup of the warm milk mixture and the plain yogurt. Whisk until smooth. Next, slowly pour the milk-yogurt mixture into the saucepan, stirring constantly.

4. Pour prepared mixture into canning jars and place them in a crock pot. Pour enough lukewarm water into the crock pot. Water need to reach just over halfway up sides of your filled jars.

5. Cook on HIGH for 5 minutes. Then, allow to stand about 4 hours, until the mixture is thick. It's important to turn on your crock pot to high for 5 minutes, every hour.

6. Chill the yogurt at least 4 hours or until yogurt is set. Store in the refrigerator and serve with your favourite croissants. Enjoy!

Cranberry Coconut Steel Cut Oatmeal

(Ready in about 6 hours | Servings 8)

Ingredients

- 2 cups steel-cut oats

- 4 cups water

- 2 cups coconut water

- 1/2 cup almonds, chopped

- 1 tablespoon brown sugar

- 1/2 teaspoon ground cinnamon

- 1/2 teaspoon salt

- 1/4 cup dried cranberries

- 1/4 cup snipped apricots

- Shredded coconut for garnish

Directions

1. In a crock pot, combine together oats, water, coconut water, almonds, sugar, cinnamon, and salt. Cover; cook on low-heat setting approximately 6 hours.

2. Top each serving with cranberries, apricots, and coconut and serve warm.

Overnight Oatmeal with Dried Fruits

(Ready in about 6 hours | Servings 8)

Ingredients

- 2 cups steel cut oats

- 1 cup raisins

- 1 cup dried cherries

- 1 cup dried figs

- 8 cups water

- 1 cup half-and-half

Directions

1. Into a crock pot, put all of the ingredients.

2. Set the crock pot to low heat and cover with a lid.

3. Cook overnight or 8 to 9 hours.

Orange Poppy Seed Bread

(Ready in about 2 hours | Servings 12)

Ingredients

- Non-stick cooking spray

- 1/4 cup poppy seeds

- 2 cups flour, all-purpose of choice

- 1 tablespoon baking soda

- 1 tablespoon honey

- 3/4 cup brown sugar

- 1/2 teaspoon kosher salt

- 3 large-sized eggs

- 1/2 cup canola oil

- 1/2 cup sour cream

- 1/4 cup whole milk

- 1 teaspoon orange zest

- 1/4 cup fresh orange juice

• 1 teaspoon vanilla extract

Directions

1. Coat a crock pot with non-stick cooking spray.

2. In a bowl, stir together poppy seeds, flour, and baking soda, and set aside.

3. In another bowl, combine together honey, sugar, salt, eggs, canola oil, sour cream, whole milk, orange zest, orange juice, and the 1 teaspoon of vanilla extract. Add this orange mixture to poppy seeds mixture. Stir to combine and place in the prepared crock pot.

4. Cover and cook on high for about 2 hours.

5. Cool completely before serving time and enjoy with freshly squeezed orange juice.

Bacon and Veggie Quiche

(Ready in about 5 hours | Servings 6)

Ingredients

- Disposable slow cooker liner

- 4 slices bacon

- 1 tablespoon olive oil

- 1 red bell pepper, chopped

- 1 green bell pepper, chopped

- 2 cups mushrooms, chopped

- 1 cup spinach

- 1 ½ cups Swiss cheese, shredded

- 2 cups whole milk

- 8 large-sized eggs

- 1 teaspoon granulated garlic

- 1 tablespoon fresh basil

- 1 teaspoon fine sea salt

- 1/4 teaspoon cayenne pepper

- 1/4 teaspoon ground black pepper

- 1/2 cup biscuit mix

Directions

1. Line your crock pot with disposable slow cooker liner.

2. In a saucepan, fry bacon slices until crisp; drain and crumble.

3. In same saucepan, heat olive oil over medium-low heat. Sauté bell pepper and mushrooms until tender. Stir in spinach and Swiss cheese.

4. In a mixing bowl, combine milk, eggs, granulated garlic, basil, salt, cayenne pepper, and black pepper. Add this mixture to mushroom mixture in the saucepan.

5. Next, fold in biscuit mix. Replace prepared mixture from the saucepan to the crock pot. Scatter the crumbled bacon on top.

6. Cover with a lid; cook on low-heat setting for 5 hours. Cool slightly before serving time, divide among serving plates and enjoy!

Spiced Oatmeal with Nuts

(Ready in about 8 hours | Servings 4)

Ingredients

- 1 cup steel cut oats

- 1 tablespoon butter

- 1/4 teaspoon turmeric powder

- 1/2 teaspoon allspice

- 2 tablespoons maple syrup

- 1 cup dried figs

- 1 cup dried apricots

- 2 cups water

- 2 cups coconut water

- 1/2 cup half-and-half

- 1/2 teaspoon sea salt

Directions

1. Combine all ingredients in your crock pot.

2. Cover the crock pot with a lid. Cook 8 hours on low or 4 hours on high-heat setting.

3. Serve with chopped nuts of choice!

Ham and Cheese Family Delight

(Ready in about 4 hours | Servings 6)

Ingredients

- Non-stick cooking spray

- 1 cup whole milk

- 2 cups light cream

- 4 eggs

- 1 red bell pepper, chopped

- 1 yellow bell pepper, chopped

- 1 onion, finely chopped

- 1 teaspoon dried basil

- 1/4 teaspoon turmeric powder

- 1 teaspoon dried thyme, crushed

- 1/2 cayenne pepper

- 1/4 teaspoon ground black pepper

- 6 cups toasted bread cubes

- 1 cup cooked ham, chopped

- 1/2 cup hard cheese, cubed

- 1/3 cup dried tomatoes

Directions

1. Lightly oil a crock pot with cooking spray.

2. In a bowl, whisk together milk, light cream, and eggs. Stir in red bell pepper, yellow bell pepper, onion, basil, turmeric, thyme, cayenne pepper and ground black pepper.

3. Next, add bread cubes, ham, cheese and tomatoes. Add the mixture to the crock pot.

4. Cook on low heat setting for about 4 hours or until a toothpick (knife) inserted in centre comes out clean. Enjoy!

Halloween Bread with Cranberries

(Ready in about 2 hours | Servings 8)

Ingredients

- Non-stick cooking spray

- 3/4 cup canned pumpkin

- 1/2 cup half-and-half

- 2 tablespoons sugar

- 1 teaspoon ground cinnamon

- 1/4 teaspoon cardamom

- 1/4 teaspoon allspice

- 2 cups all-purpose flour

- 1 teaspoon baking soda

- 1 teaspoon baking powder

- 1/2 teaspoon salt

- 1/4 cup unsalted butter, cubed

- 1/2 cup cranberries

- 1/2 cup maple syrup

- 2 tablespoons butter, melted

- 1/2 cup chopped walnuts, toasted

Directions

1. Grease your crock pot with non-stick cooking spray.

2. In a mixing bowl, combine pumpkin with half-and-half, sugar and spices.

3. In a large bowl, stir together the 2 cups of flour, the baking soda, baking powder, and salt. Next, cut in cold butter. Add pumpkin mixture to prepared flour mixture. Gently stir to combine.

4. Fold cranberries into the batter.

5. Spoon mixture into your crock pot. Pour maple syrup and melted butter over the batter. Then, scatter the walnuts over the top.

6. Cook on high-heat setting for about 2 hours. Serve warm.

Bread Pudding with Dried Figs

(Ready in about 3 hours | Servings 6)

Ingredients

- 8 cups bread cubes of choice

- 1/2 cup dried figs, chopped

- 4 medium-sized eggs

- 2 cups whole milk

- 1/4 cup butter, melted

- 1 teaspoon honey

- 1/4 cup brown sugar

- 1/4 teaspoon mint extract

- 1/4 teaspoon ground cinnamon

Directions

1. Put prepared bread cubes together with dried figs into a crock pot.

2. In a large mixing bowl, whisk together eggs, milk, butter, honey, brown sugar, mint extract, and cinnamon. Pour this mixture into the crock pot. Toss to coat.

3. Cook on low heat setting about 3 hours.

Spiced Apple Bread Pudding

(Ready in about 3 hours | Servings 8)

Ingredients

- 4 medium-sized apples, cored and chopped

- 3 cups bread, cubed

- 3 large-sized eggs

- 3/4 cup packed brown sugar

- 1/4 teaspoon allspice

- 1/2 teaspoon ground cloves

- 1 teaspoon ground cinnamon

- 1 teaspoon nutmeg

- 2 (12 fluid ounce) cans evaporated milk

Directions

1. Lay apples and bread cubes in a crock pot.

2. In a bowl, beat eggs until frothy. Stir in remaining ingredients and mix to combine.

3. Pour prepared egg mixture over apples and bread in the crock pot.

4. Cook on high heat setting for 4 hours or until custard forms.

Grandma's Apple Oatmeal

(Ready in about 6 hours | Servings 8)

Ingredients

- Margarine, melted

- 8 cups water

- 4 cups applesauce, unsweetened

- 1 1/2 cups steel cut oats

- 2 medium-sized apples, diced

- Grated nutmeg to taste

- Cardamom to taste

- Ground cinnamon to taste

- 2 tablespoons honey

Directions

1. Lightly grease your crock pot with margarine.

2. Combine the rest of ingredients in a large mixing bowl. Pour this mixture into the crock pot.

3. Cook on low heat setting at least 6 hours.

Chocolate Kid Friendly Oatmeal

(Ready in about 6 hours | Servings 10)

Ingredients

- Non-stick cooking spray

- 10 cups water

- 6 bananas, mashed

- 2 tablespoons chia seeds

- 7-8 dried dates

- 2 cups steel-cut oats

- 1 teaspoon ground cinnamon

- 1/2 cup cocoa powder, unsweetened

Directions

1. Lightly oil a crock pot with cooking spray.

2. Mix remaining ingredients in prepared crock pot.

3. Cook on low heat setting approximately 6 hours.

Vanilla Blueberry Quinoa

(Ready in about 6 hours | Servings 6)

Ingredients

- 4 cups vanilla flavoured almond milk

- 4 cups water

- 2 cups quinoa

- 2 cups blueberries

- 1/4 teaspoon grated nutmeg

- 1/4 teaspoon ground cinnamon

- 1/3 cup flax seeds

- 1/3 cup brown sugar

Directions

1. Stir all of the ingredients together in a crock pot.

2. Cover with a lid; cook on Low for 8 hours or overnight.

Apple Orange Quinoa

(Ready in about 8 hours | Servings 6)

Ingredients

- 2 cups water

- 1 cup quinoa

- 1 tablespoon fresh orange juice

- 2 cups apple juice

- 1 tablespoon chia seeds

- 1 teaspoon ground cinnamon

- 1/4 teaspoon grated nutmeg

- 1 cup raisins

- 1 teaspoon vanilla extract

Directions

1. Combine all ingredients together in your crock pot.

2. Cover with a lid; cook on low heat setting 6 to 8 hours.

Easy Yummy Breakfast Casserole

(Ready in about 12 hours | Servings 8)

Ingredients

- 1 (32-ounce) bag hash browns, frozen

- 2 carrots, thinly sliced

- 1 yellow onion, chopped

- 3 cloves garlic, minced

- 1 pound cooked ham

- 2 cups cheddar cheese, shredded

- 8 eggs

- 1 cup whole milk

- 1 teaspoon sea salt

- 1/4 teaspoon ground black pepper

- 1/4 teaspoon crushed red pepper

Directions

1. In a crock pot, alternate layers as follows: 1/2 of the hash browns, 1/2 of the carrots, 1/2 of the onions, 1/2 of the garlic, 1/2 of the cooked ham, and 1/2 of the cheddar cheese. Repeat one more time.

2. In a mixing bowl, beat the eggs; then add remaining ingredients.

3. Pour this mixture into the crockpot; cover; cook on low for 10 to 12 hours.

Restaurant Style Hash Browns

(Ready in about 3 hours | Servings 10)

Ingredients

- 1 (32-ounce) bag hash brown potatoes

- 1 pound turkey bacon, cooked

- 1 jalapeño pepper, minced

- 3 cloves garlic, crushed

- 1 cup spring onions, diced

- 1 cup Cheddar cheese

- 1 cup whole milk

- 12 eggs

- 1 teaspoon salt

- 1/2 teaspoon ground black pepper

- 1 teaspoon dried thyme

Directions

1. In your crock pot, alternate layers as follows: 1/2 of hash browns, 1/2 of bacon, 1/2 of jalapeño pepper, 1/2 of garlic, 1/2 of onions, 1/2 of cheese.

2. Next, add layers as follows: 1/2 of hash browns, 1/2 of bacon, 1/2 of jalapeño pepper, 1/2 of garlic, 1/2 of onions, 1/2 of cheese.

3. In a mixing bowl, combine milk, egg, salt, black pepper, and thyme. Pour this mixture into the crock pot.

4. Cook on low for 8 hours or overnight.

Creamy Coconut Oatmeal with Pumpkin Seeds

(Ready in about 8 hours | Servings 12)

Ingredients

- 4 cups steel cut oatmeal

- 2 cans coconut milk

- 10 cups water

- 1/4 teaspoon cardamom

- 1/2 teaspoon ground cinnamon

- 1 teaspoon almond extract

- 3 tablespoons coconut sugar

- 1/2 cup coconut flakes, for garnish

- Pumpkin seeds for garnish

Directions

1. In your crock pot, place oatmeal, coconut milk, water, cardamom, cinnamon, almond extract, and coconut sugar.

2. Turn to low and cook for about 8 hours, or until creamy.

3. Garnish with coconut flakes and pumpkin seeds!

Vanilla Almond Steel Cut Oats

(Ready in about 8 hours | Servings 12)

Ingredients

- 2 cups vanilla flavoured almond milk

- 2 cups steel cut oatmeal

- 8 cups water

- 1 teaspoon ground cinnamon

- 1/2 teaspoon grated nutmeg

- 1/4 teaspoon ground cloves

- 1 teaspoon vanilla extract

- 3 tablespoons maple syrup

- Raisins for garnish

- Chia seeds for garnish

Directions

1. In your crock pot, place almond milk, steel cut oatmeal, water, cinnamon, nutmeg, cloves, vanilla extract, and maple syrup.

2. Set the crock pot to low and cook your oatmeal for about 8 hours.

3. Garnish with raisins and chia seeds and enjoy!

Yummy Winter Breakfast

(Ready in about 3 hours | Servings 12)

Ingredients

- Non-stick cooking spray

- 1 (26-ounce) package hash brown potatoes

- 2 cups sausages

- 2 cups Cheddar cheese, shredded

- 10 eggs

- 1 cup milk

- 1/2 teaspoon dried tarragon

- 1 tablespoon granulated garlic

- 1/4 teaspoon ground black pepper

- 1 teaspoon salt

Directions

1. Oil your crock pot with cooking spray. Place hash brown potatoes in the bottom of the crock pot.

2. Heat a cast-iron skillet over medium-high flame. Then, cook sausage until they are browned, about 6 minutes. Then, spread cooked sausage over the hash brown potatoes.

3. Place shredded cheese on top.

4. In a large mixing bowl, beat the eggs with milk until frothy. Add spices and whisk to combine. Pour this mixture over the layers in the crock pot.

5. Cook for 6 to 8 hours on low-heat setting. Serve hot!

Cheesy Hash brown Casserole

(Ready in about 8 hours | Servings 6)

Ingredients

- 4 Bratwurst sausages, cooked

- 2 cups hash brown potatoes

- 1 cup sharp cheese, shredded

- 1 cup whole milk

- 4 large-sized eggs

- 1 tablespoon granulated garlic

- 1/4 teaspoon ground black pepper

- 1 teaspoon salt

- 1 teaspoon dry mustard

Directions

1. In a saucepan, cook the sausages until they are no longer pink. Place hash brown potatoes in a crock pot.

2. Transform cooked sausages to the crock pot together with their grease. Lay sharp cheese on top.

3. In a mixing bowl, combine the rest of ingredients. Pour this egg mixture into the crock pot.

4. Cook on low for about 8 hours, or overnight. Serve with mustard and sour cream.

Thanksgiving Bacon Casserole

(Ready in about 10 hours | Servings 10)

Ingredients

- 1 tablespoon olive oil

- 1 cup green onions, chopped

- 1 green bell pepper, thinly sliced

- 1 red bell pepper, thinly sliced

- 2 cloves garlic, minced

- 2 pounds hash brown potatoes, frozen and thawed

- 8 slices turkey bacon, cooked

- 1 1/2 cups Gouda, shredded

- 10 large-sized eggs

- 1 cup milk

- 1/4 teaspoon cayenne pepper

- 1 teaspoon sea salt

- 1/4 teaspoon ground black pepper

- 1 heaping tablespoon fresh parsley

- 1/4 cup chives

Directions

1. In a cast-iron skillet, heat olive oil over medium flame. Sauté green onions, bell peppers, and garlic until green onions are softened. Stir in hash brown potatoes and cook for 2 more minutes.

2. Lay 1/2 of the onion-potato mixture in your crock pot; then, lay 1/2 of the cooked bacon and top with 1/2 of shredded Gouda cheese.

3. Repeat layering in the same manner.

4. Whisk eggs together with remaining ingredients; pour this egg mixture over cheese layer in the crock pot.

5. Cook on low heat setting, 8 to 10 hours.

Amazing Spiced Omelette

(Ready in about 2 hours | Servings 4)

Ingredients

- 6 eggs

- 1/2 cup whole milk

- 1 teaspoon sea salt

- 1/4 teaspoon freshly ground black pepper

- 1 teaspoon dried basil

- 1 teaspoon dried oregano

- 1 teaspoon dried thyme

- 1/4 teaspoon chili powder

- 1 small head of cauliflower, broken into florets

- 1 medium-sized red onion, chopped

- 1 garlic clove, minced

- 1 cup Cheddar cheese, shredded

- Chives for garnish

• Olives for garnish

Directions

1. Lightly oil the inside of your crock pot.

2. In a mixing bowl or a measuring cup, whisk the eggs, milk, and spices. Mix until everything is well combined.

3. Add cauliflower florets, onions and garlic to crock pot. Add the spiced egg mixture.

4. Cover; then, cook on high approximately 2 hours, or until eggs are set.

5. Scatter shredded cheese on top and place a lid; let stand until cheddar cheese is melted.

6. Divide the omelette into wedges, garnish with chives and olives and serve.

Overnight Western Omelette

(Ready in about 12 hours | Servings 12)

Ingredients

- 2 pounds hash brown potatoes

- 1 cup spinach

- 1 pound cooked ham, sliced

- 2 cloves garlic, minced

- 1 yellow onion, diced

- 1 red bell pepper, seeded and diced

- 1 cup Gouda cheese, shredded

- 10 eggs

- 1 ½ cup milk

- 1 teaspoon sea salt

- 1/4 teaspoon freshly ground black pepper

- 1/4 teaspoon chili powder

Directions

1. Lightly oil your crock pot with non-stick cooking spray.

2. Alternate layers in your crock pot. Place 1/3 of the hash brown potatoes; place 1/3 of the spinach; then place 1/3 of cooked ham, 1/3 of garlic, 1/3 of the onion and 1/3 of bell pepper.

3. Top with shredded Gouda cheese; repeat same layers two more times.

4. In a large-sized bowl, mix together remaining ingredients. Pour in the crock pot.

5. Cover with a lid; cook on low-heat setting for 10 to 12 hours. Serve with toasted bread and mustard.

Vegetable and Ham Casserole

(Ready in about 8 hours | Servings 4)

Ingredients

- 1/4 cup extra-virgin olive oil

- 1 parsnip, peeled and chopped

- 1 turnip, peeled and chopped

- 2 cloves garlic, minced

- 1 cup ham, cooked and diced

- 3/4 cup whole milk

- 4 large-sized eggs

- 1/4 teaspoon turmeric

- 1/2 teaspoon rosemary

- 1/4 teaspoon dried thyme

- 1 tablespoon heaping fresh parsley

- Croutons for garnish

Directions

1. In your crock pot, combine together first four ingredients. Top with ham.

2. In a bowl, whisk together milk, eggs, and spices. Pour over the vegetables and ham in the crock pot.

3. Cook on low for 6 to 8 hours. Serve with croutons.

Creamy Oatmeal with Berries

(Ready in about 8 hours | Servings 4)

Ingredients

- 1 cup oats

- 1/2 teaspoon allspice

- 2 cups water

- 1 cup coconut water

- 1 pinch of grated nutmeg

- 1 pinch of ground cinnamon

- 1 pinch of salt

- 1 cup half-and-half cream

- 1/4 cup brown sugar

- Berries of choice, for garnish

Directions

1. Simply put all ingredients together (except berries) into your crock pot, just before going to bed.

2. Set the crock pot on low and cook overnight.

3. Serve with your favourite berries or mixed berries and enjoy warm!

Vegan Steel-Cut Oatmeal

(Ready in about 3 hours | Servings 6)

Ingredients

- 2 bananas, mashed

- 1 cup coconut water

- 4 cups water, divided

- 1 cup steel cut oats

- 1/4 cup dried figs

- 1/4 cup dried cranberries

- 1 teaspoon vanilla extract

- 1/2 teaspoon cardamom

- 1/2 teaspoon ground cinnamon

- Coconut sugar to taste

Directions

1. Purée bananas in your blender; then transfer mashed bananas to a crock pot.

2. Add remaining ingredients.

3. Cook on medium heat setting for 3 hours. Remember to stir every 30 minutes.

4. Serve with additional fruit if desired and enjoy!

Pumpkin Steel Cut Oats

(Ready in about 6 hours | Servings 6)

Ingredients

- Non-stick cooking spray

- 6 cups water

- 1 ½ cups steel-cut oats

- 1/2 cup brown sugar

- 1 (15-ounce) can pumpkin puree

- 1 teaspoon vanilla extract

- 1 teaspoon cardamom

- 1 tablespoon pumpkin pie spice

- 1 teaspoon ground cinnamon

Directions

1. Grease your crock pot with cooking spray.

2. Place all of the ingredients.

3. Cook on low for 6 hours. Divide among six serving bowls, sprinkle with pumpkin seeds and serve.

Mouth Watering French Toast Casserole

(Ready in about 5 hours | Servings 8)

Ingredients

- 2 bread loaves, cut into bite-sized cubes

- 1 teaspoon lemon zest

- 6 large-sized eggs

- 1 ½ cups milk

- 1 teaspoon pure almond extract

- 1 cup half-and-half

- 1/4 teaspoon grated nutmeg

- 1/4 teaspoon ground cloves

- 1 teaspoon ground cinnamon

- 1 cup brown sugar

- 3 tablespoons butter, melted

- 2 cups slivered almonds

Directions

1. Grease a crock pot with non-stick spray or with a melted butter.

2. Preheat the oven to 225 degrees F. Place prepared bread cubes on a cookie sheet and bake for about 30 minutes, or until the bread cubes are dried.

3. Lay the bread cubes on the bottom of your crock pot.

4. Mix together lemon zest, eggs, milk, almond extract, half-and-half, nutmeg, cloves, and cinnamon. Pour this mixture over the bread cubes in the crock pot.

5. In a separate small-sized bowl, combine the brown sugar, butter, and almonds. Stir in your crock pot.

6. Set crock pot to low; cover and cook approximately 5 hours.

7. Serve with fruits and maple syrup if desired.

Tater Tot Breakfast Casserole

(Ready in about 8 hours | Servings 8)

Ingredients

- 1 (30-ounces) package tater tots

- 1 cup bacon

- 1 cup green onions, chopped

- 2 cups sharp cheese, shredded

- 12 eggs

- 1 cup whole milk

- 3 tablespoons all-purpose flour

- 1/4 teaspoon ground black pepper

- 1/4 teaspoon cayenne pepper

- 1 teaspoon kosher salt

Directions

1. In a greased crock pot, place 1/3 of the tater tots, then, 1/3 of the bacon, 1/3 of green onions and finally, add 1/3 of shredded cheeses. Repeat these layers two more times, ending with the cheese.

2. In a large-sized bowl, whisk together the rest of ingredients; add to the crock pot.

3. Cover the crock pot and set on low; then, cook 6 to 8 hours.

Soft and Yummy Buttermilk Bread

(Ready in about 3 hours | Servings 8)

Ingredients

- 1 ½ cups all-purpose flour

- 1 teaspoon baking soda

- 1 teaspoon baking powder

- A pinch of salt

- 4 tablespoons butter, cut into pieces

- A pinch of grated nutmeg

- 3/4 cup buttermilk

Directions

1. In a large-sized mixing bowl, combine all-purpose flour, baking soda, baking powder, and salt; cut in butter until this mixture resembles small crumbs.

2. Stir in grated nutmeg and buttermilk.

3. Knead dough and then pat it into greased springform pan.

4. Place on a rack; cover and cook on high for about 2 ½ hours. Serve with milk.

Delicious Herb Bread

(Ready in about 3 hours | Servings 8)

Ingredients

- 1 ½ cups all-purpose flour

- 1 teaspoon baking powder

- 1 teaspoon baking soda

- 1 teaspoon dried dill weed

- 1 teaspoon ground black pepper

- 1 tablespoon dried chives

- A pinch of salt

- 4 tablespoons cold margarine, cut into pieces

- 3/4 cup buttermilk

Directions

1. In a mixing bowl, combine first seven ingredients. Then, cut in cold margarine until the mixture resembles small crumbs.

2. Stir in buttermilk and replace the dough on the floured surface.

3. Knead your dough for about 3 minutes.

4. Place on a rack and bake on high for about 2 hours. Serve warm and enjoy with cheese.

Cranberry-Raisin Bran Bread

(Ready in about 3 hours | Servings 16)

Ingredients

- 1/2 cup whole-wheat flour

- 1 ½ cups all-purpose flour

- 1 teaspoons baking powder

- 1 teaspoon baking soda

- 1 teaspoon pumpkin pie spice

- 1 teaspoon allspice

- 1/4 teaspoon grated nutmeg

- 1/2 teaspoon salt

- 1 ½ cups whole-bran cereal flakes

- 2 cups buttermilk

- 1/4 cup maple syrup

- 3 tablespoons butter, melted

- 2 eggs

- 1/2 cup dried cranberries, coarsely chopped

- 1/2 cup raisins, coarsely chopped

- 1/4 cup pecans, chopped

- 1/4 walnuts, chopped

Directions

1. In a large-sized mixing bowl, combine first nine ingredients until everything is well combined.

2. Next, add buttermilk, maple syrup, butter, eggs; stir to combine.

3. Gently fold in dried cranberries, raisins, pecans and walnuts.

4. Pour prepared dough into greased and floured loaf pan.

5. Bake on high for about 3 hours, or until a toothpick (or a knife) inserted in centre of your loaf comes out clean.

6. Serve with fruit jam or honey!

Sloppy Joe-Style Burgers

(Ready in about 3 hours | Servings 12)

Ingredients

- 2 pounds lean beef, ground

- 1 yellow onion, finely chopped

- 1 zucchini, chopped

- 1 yellow bell pepper, chopped

- 1 red bell pepper, chopped

- 1 cup button mushrooms, sliced

- 1/2 cup fried bacon, crumbled

- 1 teaspoon garlic powder

- 1/2 teaspoon chili powder

- 3/4 cup tomato paste

- 1 cup reduced-fat cheese, cubed

- 2 bay leaves

- 1 teaspoon sea salt

- 1/4 teaspoon ground black pepper

- 12 burger buns

Directions

1. In a large saucepan or a wok, over medium flame, cook ground beef with onion, zucchini and bell peppers. Cook until ground beef is browned.

2. Add to the slow cooker and then stir in remaining ingredients (except buns).

3. Cook on low for 2 to 3 hours. Serve on burger buns and add pickles if desired.

Nutty Granola with Coconut Oil

(Ready in about 2 hours 30 minutes | Servings 12)

Ingredients

- Cooking spray

- 4 cups rolled oats, old fashioned

- 1 cup almonds, chopped

- 1/2 cup pecans, chopped

- 1/2 teaspoon allspice

- 1 teaspoon cinnamon

- A pinch of salt

- 1/2 cup maple syrup

- 1/2 cup coconut oil, melted

- 1/4 cup brown sugar

- 1 teaspoon pure almond extract

Directions

1. Oil your crock pot with cooking spray. Add the rolled oats and reserve.

2. Add the almonds and pecans.

3. In a mixing bowl, whisk together remaining ingredients.

4. Pour this mixture over the oats and nuts in the crock pot.

5. Cook approximately 2 hours on low, stirring every 30 minutes.

6. Spread prepared granola out on a sheet of aluminium foil and let it cool.

Herbed Chili Cornbread

(Ready in about 2 hours | Servings 8)

Ingredients

- 3/4 cup all-purpose flour

- 1/4 cup cornmeal

- 1 tablespoon sugar

- 1 teaspoon baking soda

- 1 teaspoon baking powder

- 1 teaspoon dried basil

- 1 teaspoon ground cumin

- 1/2 teaspoon dried oregano

- 1/2 teaspoon salt

- 1 large-sized egg, beaten

- 1/2 cup buttermilk

- 1/4 poblano pepper, cooked and minced

- 1/4 cup whole kernel corn

Directions

1. Combine first ten ingredients in a large-sized mixing bowl.

2. Stir in buttermilk, poblano and corn and. Stir well to combine.

3. Transfer the dough to greased and floured baking pan

4. Next, place this baking pan on a rack in your crock pot. Cover; cook on high-heat setting approximately 2 hours.

5. Allow to cool for about 10 minutes before serving time.

Caramel Flavored Banana Bread

(Ready in about 2 hours | Servings 8)

Ingredients

- 4 tablespoons butter, melted

- 1⁄4 cup applesauce

- 2 medium-sized eggs

- 1 tablespoon water

- 1 tablespoon milk

- 3⁄4 cup brown sugar

- 3 ripe bananas, mashed

- 1 ¾ cups all-purpose flour

- 1 teaspoon baking powder

- 1 teaspoon baking soda

- 1⁄4 teaspoon salt

- 1⁄4 cup almonds, coarsely chopped

Directions

1. In a bowl, beat butter, applesauce, eggs, water, milk, and brown sugar until creamy and uniform.

2. Add mashed bananas, flour, baking powder, baking soda, and salt. Stir in almonds.

3. Pour batter into suitable loaf pan.

4. Cook on high for about 3 hours until a toothpick (or knife) inserted in centre of your banana bread comes out clean.

5. Remove banana bread from loaf pan and cool to room temperature.

Pumpkin-Almond Bread

(Ready in about 3 hours 30 minutes | Servings 16)

Ingredients

- 1 cup pumpkin, canned

- 4 tablespoons margarine, melted

- 1/2 cup granulated sugar

- 2 medium-sized eggs, beaten

- 1/2 cup milk

- 2 cups all-purpose flour

- 1 teaspoon baking powder

- 1 teaspoon baking soda

- 1/4 teaspoon grated nutmeg

- 1 teaspoon pumpkin pie spice

- A pinch of salt

- 1/2 cup almonds, toasted and chopped

Directions

1. In a large-sized bowl, combine pumpkin with margarine and sugar until well blended; stir in eggs and milk.

2. Add flour, baking powder, baking soda, nutmeg, pumpkin pie spice, and salt; mix in chopped almonds.

3. Spoon batter into loaf pan and place in your crock pot. Cook on high about 3 ½ hours.

4. Allow your pumpkin bread to cool on a wire rack. Serve with honey and enjoy!

Cheesy Rosemary Bread

(Ready in about 2 hours | Servings 8)

Ingredients

- 6 tablespoons butter, room temperature

- 1 cup grated Parmesan cheese

- 1 tablespoon fresh rosemary

- 1 medium-sized loaf bread

Directions

1. Combine butter, Parmesan cheese and fresh rosemary and mix until everything is well blended.

2. Cut loaf bread into 8 slices. Spread both sides of bread slices with rosemary-cheese mixture.

3. Wrap bread slices in an aluminium foil.

4. Place in your crock pot and cook on low-heat setting for 2 hours. Uncover and allow to cool for about 5 minutes.

Vegetarian Sloppy Joes

(Ready in about 3 hours | Servings 8)

Ingredients

- 1 cup mushrooms, thinly sliced

- 1 cup onion, chopped

- 1 red bell pepper, chopped

- 1/4 poblano pepper, minced

- 2 teaspoons minced garlic

- 1 cup tomato catsup

- 1 teaspoon celery seeds

- 1 ½ cup water

- 1/4 cup sugar

- 1 teaspoon kosher salt

- 1/4 ground black pepper

- 8 whole-wheat hamburger buns

Directions

1. Combine mushrooms, onions, bell pepper, poblano pepper, garlic, catsup, celery seeds, water, and sugar.

2. Cover your crock pot with a lid and cook Sloppy Joes on high 2 to 3 hours. Season with salt and pepper.

3. Serve in buns with your favourite salad.

Deluxe Beef Sandwiches

(Ready in about 3 hours | Servings 12)

Ingredients

- 2 pounds lean ground beef

- 1 red bell pepper, chopped

- 1 green bell pepper, chopped

- 1 yellow onion, chopped

- 1 cup mushrooms, thinly sliced

- 2 cloves garlic, minced

- 1/2 cup fried turkey bacon, crumbled

- 3/4 cup tomato paste

- 1 tablespoon tomato catsup

- 2 tablespoons dry red wine

- 1 cup processed cheese, cubed

- Salt and pepper, to taste

- 12 sandwich buns, toaste

Directions

1. Heat a large skillet over medium heat; cook ground beef, bell peppers and onion until meat is browned and onion is translucent. Replace to the crock pot.

2. Add remaining ingredients, except sandwich buns; cook on low-heat setting for about 3 hours.

3. Serve on sandwich buns, garnish with mustard and salad and enjoy.

Best-ever Meat Sandwiches

(Ready in about 3 hours | Servings 12)

Ingredients

- 1 pound mixed beef and pork, ground

- 3/4 cup spring onions, chopped

- 1 clove garlic, minced

- 1 cup tomatoes, diced and drained

- 1 tablespoon Worcestershire sauce

- 1/4 cup packed light brown sugar

- 1 tablespoon mustard

- 1 heaping tablespoon cilantro

- 1 heaping tablespoon fresh parsley

- 1 teaspoon sea salt

- 1/4 teaspoon ground black pepper

- 1/4 teaspoon red pepper, crushed

- 12 sandwich rolls, toasted

Directions

1. In a wide and deep saucepan, over medium-low flame, cook mixed meat, spring onion, and garlic; crumble with a fork; add to the crock pot.

2. Add the rest of ingredients, except sandwich rolls; cook on high 2 to 3 hours.

3. Arrange sandwiches with rolls and serve with some extra ketchup and mustard.

BBQ Chicken Sandwiches

(Ready in about 8 hours | Servings 8)

Ingredients

- 1 pound chicken breasts, boneless and skinless

- 1/2 cup chicken stock

- 1/4 cup BBQ sauce

- 1/4 cup water

- 1 cup catsup

- 2 tablespoons white dry wine

- 1/3 cup yellow mustard

- 1 teaspoon tarragon

- 1 celery stalk, chopped

- 1 large-sized carrot, chopped

- 2 tablespoons brown sugar

- 1/2 cup chopped onion

- 1 clove garlic, minced

• Salt and pepper, to taste

• 8 hamburger buns

Directions

1. In your crock pot, combine all of the ingredients, except hamburger buns.

2. Cover with a lid and cook on low 6 to 8 hours, or overnight. Next, shred cooked chicken, adjust seasoning and serve with buns.

Saucy Pork Sandwiches

(Ready in about 8 hours | Servings 12)

Ingredients

For the Sandwiches:

- 1 pork loin roast, boneless

- 1 teaspoon garlic powder

- 1 teaspoon onion powder

- 1/4 teaspoon ground black pepper

- Sea salt to taste

- 1/2 cup water

- 12 sandwich buns

For the Sauce:

- 1 cup reduced-fat mayonnaise

- 1 clove garlic, minced

- 2 tablespoons lemon juice

Directions

1. Rub pork loin with garlic pcwder, onion powder, ground black pepper and salt to taste. Pour in water. Place in a crock pot and cook on low-heat setting overnight, or about 8 hours.

2. Remove pork from the crock pot and shred it.

3. Mix all ingredients for the sauce.

4. Spoon cooked pork onto bottoms of sandwich buns. Then spoon prepared sauce and place top of the buns. Enjoy!

Summer Granola with Seeds

(Ready in about 2 hours | Servings 16)

Ingredients

- 6 cups oats, old-fashioned

- 1 cup pumpkin seeds

- 1 cup sunflower kernels

- 1/2 teaspoon kosher salt

- 2 tablespoons orange juice

- 1/2 cup canola oil

- 1 cup maple syrup

- 1/2 cup dried figs, chopped

- 1 cup dried pineapple, chopped

Directions

1. In a crock pot, combine together oats, pumpkin seeds, sunflower kernels, and salt.

2. In a small-sized bowl, whisk orange juice, oil and maple syrup until mixture is blended. Stir this mixture into oat mixture.

3. Cook, covered, on high-heat setting for about 2 hours, stirring every 20 minutes.

4. Remove from the heat and let granola cool. Add dried figs and pineapple and stir well to combine.

5. Place prepared granola on a baking sheets, spreading evenly. Cool completely before storing.

Easy-to-make Date Granola

(Ready in about 3 hours | Servings 6)

Ingredients

- 1/4 cup honey

- 6 tablespoons applesauce

- 1/4 teaspoon cardamom

- 1/4 teaspoon grated nutmeg

- 1/4 teaspoon ground cloves

- 1 teaspoon ground cinnamon

- A pinch of salt

- 1 teaspoon vanilla extract

- 1/2 teaspoon maple extract

- 1 tablespoon hemp seeds

- 3 cups rolled oats

- 1 cup walnuts, toasted and chopped

- 1 cup Medjool dates, pitted and chopped

Directions

1. Put honey, applesauce, cardamom, nutmeg, cloves, cinnamon, salt, vanilla extract and maple extracts into your crock pot. Add hemp seeds and stir well to combine.

2. Stir in rolled oats and walnuts. Stir to combine.

3. Cook on high for 3 hours, venting the lid slightly. Stir occasionally. Allow to cool slightly and then add chopped dates.

4. Pour your granola onto a baking sheet and allow to cool completely before serving in the airtight containers.

Coconut Maple Granola

(Ready in about 3 hours | Servings 6)

Ingredients

- 1/4 cup maple syrup

- 2 tablespoons canola oil

- 1 cup hulled sunflower seeds

- 2 tablespoons chia seeds

- 1/4 teaspoon ground cloves

- 1 teaspoon ground cinnamon

- A pinch of salt

- 1 teaspoon pure vanilla extract

- 1 cup coconut flakes

- 3 cups rolled oats

- 1 cup slivered almonds

- 1 cup dried cherries, chopped

Directions

1. Combine maple syrup, canola oil, sunflower seeds, chia seeds, ground cloves, cinnamon, salt, vanilla extract, coconut flakes and rolled oats in a crock pot.

2. Cook approximately 3 hours, stirring occasionally. Allow granola to cool for about 15 minutes; add almonds and dried cherries. Stir until everything is well incorporated.

3. Spread onto a baking sheet in order to cool completely.

Pulled Pork Sandwiches

(Ready in about 3 hours | Servings 12)

Ingredients

- 1 pork loin roast, boneless

- 1 teaspoon curry powder

- 1 teaspoon cayenne pepper

- 1/2 teaspoon grated ginger

- 1 cup beef broth

- Salt to taste

- 1/4 teaspoon black pepper

- 1 bay leaf

- 48 bread slices

Directions

1. Rub pork loin roast with curry powder and cayenne pepper.

2. Place seasoned pork in your crock pot; add grated ginger and beef broth. Add salt, black pepper and bay leaf.

3. Cook on low for about 3 hours. Cut cooked pork into thin shreds. Taste and adjust the seasonings.

4. Make sandwiches spooning meat with sauce into each bread slice.

Winter Beef Sandwiches

(Ready in about 8 hours | Servings 12)

Ingredients

- 1 medium-sized beef chuck roast, boneless

- 1/2 teaspoon sea salt

- 1/4 teaspoon black pepper

- 1 teaspoon dried basil

- 1 tablespoon fresh sage

- 2 cups beef broth

- 1 cup dry red wine

- 1 clove garlic, minced

- 7-8 peppercorns

- 12 sandwich rolls

- Sauerkraut for garnish

- Chillies for garnish

Directions

1. Season beef chuck roast with sea salt and black pepper and lay in a crock pot.

2. Add basil, sage, beef broth, wine, garlic, and peppercorns. Cover and cook on low approximately 8 hours, or overnight.

3. Serve cooked beef on sandwich rolls with sauerkraut and chillies.

Lightning Source UK Ltd.
Milton Keynes UK
UKHW020631190821
389117UK00013B/1030